ALMS FOR THE BORED

SAM PEKARSKE

Alms for the Bored ©2018 by Sam Pekarske.

Published in the United States by Vegetarian Alcoholic Press. Not one part of this work may be reproduced without expressed written consent from the author. For more information, please contact vegalpress@gmail.com

ISBN 13: 978-1-7326827-1-9

Cover Art **©2018 by Chelsea Velaga**

POETRY AS AN ACT OF UNALIENABLE COMPULSION, OR TRYING TO WRITE WITH DEAD HANDS

2	alms for the bored
4	for eau claire, movement one (part two)
6	tin sluts
8	denim -- daddy
10	a sweater weather cacophony for mean people
11	uxo, xoxo
14	dust buddy meets a leftover eyelash
16	notes on talking
17	misunderstood, or a product of mishearsay
19	keeping hands on the disconnect between ghosts
21	re:
22	tell me I'm wrong / fight me
23	broken doors on swollen hinges
24	notes on marriage to wet sand
26	out of touch and on time

PEKARSKE HEAVY INDUSTRIES (SLIGHT FEARS, TREMBLING)

30	for eau claire, movement two (part four)
32	organica
33	a groundwater anthem for sloppy days
35	retrospectacular
36	forgetting, but it's complicated
37	"too turnt for earth"
38	sincerely chaotic <3
39	"did you really just say that you hate your band's music?"
41	like the sound of a few levers pulled all at once
42	an introduction to vague bile studies, tear duct harmonies
44	pissing and waning
45	we're all so undone / it's so undone
47	for swaths of time I was worth the sum of my parts, or canopy cannibalism
49	I saw you with a grass house, I saw you with a neighborly scream
51	sounds like another word for decay that the dictionary didn't need

BIPOLAR DISORDERLY CONDUCT

56	nocturnal files, movement 26
58	nocturnal files, movement 28
60	nocturnal files, movement 22
62	somnolence, a side effect
63	how 2 look most beautiful, a side effect
66	deafeningly, still, a side effect
67	disembarkment technique
68	headstudy (latent and undeveloped reveries signing off in 2011)
71	dreamscape, or "hospitality / hospitable"
72	dreamscape, or "reckoning versus reconciliation"
73	dreamscape, or "natural death"
74	dreamscape, or "night memory"
75	dreamscape, or "barbeque, barbe-you"
76	dreamscape, or "nightmare waves on a broken bed, we're spaceful and it's morning"
77	dreamscape, or "bedding / bidding / biding"

MILWAUKEE WAS BUILT ON SWAMP + BILE (AND IF YOU DON'T THINK SO, YOU'RE NOT WRONG)

80	ode to milwaukee
83	jazz man sez
85	city song, movement 2
87	gilt, guilt, etc.
88	a history of hot summers
89	fickle fucker texts a ghost
90	from mke to sdf
92	moving through bluelight

        movement one
        movement two
        movement three
        movement four
        movement five
        movement six
        movement seven
        movement eight
        movement nine
        movement ten

105	"an inspiring fight against death"
106	city song, movement 5
108	city hymn, movement 1
109	watching water, f-ish minor
110	calm press, d minor (parking structure, undefined)
112	razed in milwaukee
113	moribund

LIVING UNDER THE CONSTANT THREAT OF STARS

118	unrehearsed in place, time, and space
120	biography for something darkening
122	reconnaissance, or how insincerity is key to getting by
123	make life / think death (thumbs up)
124	widower maker faire
125	unwed handwriting
127	plaints about planes and underwater anthems
129	sometimes, still
	movement one
	movement two
	movement three
	movement four
134	the last diatribe doesn't sweat the small stuff
136	take note, all you slimy fuckers:
138	plaints 4 the dust age
139	like eyelids spitting
140	on dead friends and hoodoo
141	ornithology in a dry town
142	folkenlanguage

MY BODY IS A FRAGILE STATE, MY BODY IS A SHIP THAT SAILS UNDER MUDDIED FLAGS

146	and on this day
148	holy
150	it didn't work out and I'm not sorry for giving up
152	easy out / tunnel verse
153	"can't fit into this dang capitalist framework"
154	repose / reprise
156	a brief brush with sentimentality
157	collapse in several movements
159	exercises in creepy teethmarks
161	little litanies for small gods everywhere
162	light + wild
163	ash wednesday
164	streetlight lightbulb filaments' resolve
165	a coffin nail
166	for kris, movement 3

"SO THIS ONE'S FOR THE LOST ONES,
    AND THE DEAD ONES,
        AND THE ONES WHO FELL AWAY"

    - ASMZ

POETRY AS AN ACT OF UNALIENABLE COMPULSION, OR TRYING TO WRITE WITH DEAD HANDS

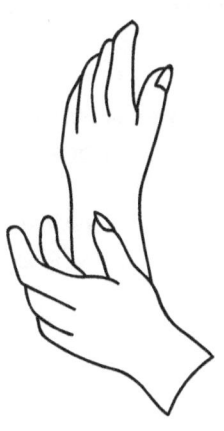

ALMS FOR THE BORED

and the liminal.

and leafless trees with hollow wood,
and the people for which that is an allegory.

and everything alive and obviously dying,
and the moral phenomenon of staying still.

and the weak of wares but rich of spirit,
and the spirits that went too soon to boot.

> *alms for all and all at once*
> *and all my alms for you, too.*

alms for the board of directors / just kidding,
alms for the poor, alms for the undercurrent,

alms in reverse for the overburdened or
an alm of removal and relief, at best.

> *one for all and all for one, or*
> *alms for all and alms for none.*

alms for the descent, how it happened so quickly,
alms for finality, how giving in becomes a relief,

and alms for all of the fuck if it matters,
alms for all of my fragile attempts to care,
and chaos organizes into careful cacophony,
and there's still no corks for the wine--

        and everything has come undone so quickly,
        and a current comes to a rest at my feet,
        and silence is quieter than it sounds at least,
        and a lot of times I can't remember my name,
        and a lot of times I sleep but can't rest, oh my,

as much of the world as I take in my fists
I tarry the loneliness of the dead in my hands,
squelching and reeling, they ask for nothing.

        so--
give alms for a total fucking abyss of the mind,
give alms for ailments and hurts of the heart,

alms and cheers and litanies and lilts,
and alms for me-- the bored and boring.

FOR EAU CLAIRE, MOVEMENT ONE (PART TWO)

understanding a desire for lawlessness
when there's enough space left to un-govern.

houses strewn with snow, built
in an effigy of unwed wind--it's breadth

speaks in such a terse ostinato-- piercingly,
she says it's been enough time between

cities, she says there's going to be something
grave tonight, says she's going to a show

and she doesn't, but she says she did,
it's softer that way, languid

and so very becoming. our legs look long
in a place without sewers, city tunnels

for the sickly creeping vanish in this place.
vanish is a word for city widows, vanish

is a place I'd go to in the bible, is a light
and irresponsibly vacant state of mind,

is a stop on the highway, is fifteen years of
snowshine, vanish is where I'd go to die

if it fits in the itinerary and out here
I reject the expanse, I resent

the chasm between swaths of highway,
grass lays about the ditch without

a hint of intent, stays there until
we are so turgid and brown I can't breathe,

I can't breathe, I won't on purpose. I said
the terror I feel in this place is ineffable,

it came out as *I'm fine* with a wash of fear.
it came out as dead eyes and no heart.

       so I said to this place--

swallow my name, I'll be home soon.

TIN SLUTS
read in a drunk country mouth tone

      imagine me--
not in, close, screaming at
a bath towel like a body
it was shaped like my breasts
so I hate it, lavishly

coat its fibers in insult
and rip the drip right off of me.

we're coral-rough now.
we dried in the sun-breeze,
we crumble like spent cells,

we're a lot less infamous than
we'd prefer to be / sex sells, but
notorious shit is forever:

ten sluts say their peace and
ten sluts ask me where the water fell,

ten sluts--ten out of ten--all bored
of your maggot prose and
gutter verse, I try

to find coke in the bible,
I try to find god in a man
who says I try real hard,

say it's 'cause he can't stay hard
    (laugh track)

but that brow look good, yeah
eyes like a dead fucking fish,
itch like benediction, that

scowl looks fresh, yeah,
wonder who's soulless disposition
you jacked to get off,

wonder why we don't dry off,
stay shaking and naked and

real mad about it.

DENIM --
-- DADDY

*"I fucked your girlfriend and I would probably do it again.
You slashed my tires and I hope that you would do it
again."*
- Why?

I said "burn the whole city down,"
told you to shut your eyes first and
open your mouth later, after we had
something better to do,

"burn the whole city down," through
clenched teeth and fists like stuck knots,

these star crossed fuckboys parading
carhartt jackets like my father wears,
nodding off to poorly syncopated beats,
burning down the left-behinds
in concrete baths

yeah,
I'll show them--

    I'll strike a match against callouses
earned over years of shoveling bullshit,

      I'll light the first couple fires
and tend to them needlessly enough,

      I'll keep crying about how
spacesuits look like white denim
and how unfortunate that must be
for 1960s americana's latent PR team

      I'll detour rush hour traffic
into the gap between your teeth-- it's hairy

      I'll dewy decimate the last few
stolen books in my wet paper armory

      I'll burn the whole city down,
and dress our wounds with wet tape,
leave the radio on, and close the doors.

when I couldn't see your dick
through a thousand rusty oracles

I asked myself-- what would jesus do
if it were in god that I trusted?

there's nothing better to do,
the radio is off, the curtains are closed,
so burn the whole city down.

A SWEATER WEATHER CACOPHONY FOR MEAN PEOPLE

hugging and fucking and touching and ringing
and hugging and fucking and touching and ringing
while cinder / smoke aisles run the gamut,
teaching my   *hands*   to jive quick enough,
teaching my   *legs*   to step brisk enough,

flowers are suckered and killed in not-light,
and my attitude is ringing with discord and whey,
little life bites your neck my neck so try to hold it.

flame smoke / water smoke / steam time,
sitting on the syncopated beats to eat the rest
I bore my forefathers with rusty blues scales,

I bore my forefathers with crimes against humility,
we cradle it / my / hour / our neck so sing the crime.

holding notes for the waxing,
singing songs of the waning,
stupid moon sounds of hugging and fucking and
touching and ringing and hugging and
fucking and touching and ringing
and party and bullshit and

...

UXO, XOXO

I think I have a body and it's
a broken machine, whirring,

I have a heart / had a heart,
and it's a fleshy fish, sleeping;

inventory of a species, I'm all
here and trying not to fight you,

I'm all here and we're all so
desperate, if a little desolate,

if not for naught for no way
can this get any better unless

it's on fire / we're all on fire /
ask me anything, I swear

I saved all of my wildest lies
for the moment you'd ask me

to keep your slacked jaw
entertained and enmeshed in the

fiber of the world / my place in
the tithes / donate my mind to

the science of sleep, calm my
memory as it sits outside of me,

calm my platitudes, my fist hand,
or rile me up with a dying promise--

> *I worked so hard for this,*
> *I worked so hard for all of this!*

fighting to be in love with the
gravel / to keep my mouth shut

at the slightest hint of grass,
pounding the entrances to the

tanks of gasoline that keep caverns
beneath their stations and pumps,

the heart of the matter / the heart
of it all, the blood of a sinkhole

is the juice of the city and the
wet of my eyelids licking back.

asleep sits a syllable away from
afraid and I can't even help it

snatch up its roots from rue and
carry it through the dictionary,

where we're all safe / we're all
saved / our neighbors are harmless.

DUST BUDDY MEETS A LEFTOVER EYELASH

these scraps of dust need rest,
even the wild eye of my perfumed
mind turns to a nap for a time,
just me and my jilted breath--

>sinking and asleep,
>it sneaks through my
>lung-meat, signaling back
>to the other dust legions--
>*this is a prime place*
>*for your collection*

>>of spider hairs,
>>of grated sinew,
>>of lucky skin cells,
>>of gray skies falling,

the dust obeys and
the curtains fall,

thrusting a million motes
into a single modicum,

        bloated and over it
        in a sticky synaptic wave,

healing my broken tides with
decorum and terse whispers,
coming clean with the other
grifters, feeling honest and grave,

having escaped the torpor,
licking lips into summer swirls--

cheers to endless eyelids and
favorable forecasts, my resolve
descends and arpeggiates over
and over, disillusioned and free.

NOTES ON TALKING

you aren't enough mouth for me,
not enough gape or maw or

piqued pieces of exposed skeleton
teeth, you aren't enough teeth

for me, you're not enough skull or
moon or meat or stars, you're a lot

less than more than enough, if
tongues were alms you'd be too few,

if I could keep language in my hands
I would, I'd lay mouths to rest, but you

already have no lips to offer, no spit
to drip along to, if all tomorrow's

textbooks fell dormant I would find the
page about mouths and scratch your

name from the record, you don't belong
in a holy archive of tooth sounds,

you're not enough mouth for me, you
aren't enough mouth for me, you're not.

MISUNDERSTOOD, OR A PRODUCT OF MISHEARSAY

these are all poems based on
the problems of being present,
how memory
                and ephemera

carry side effects of spirals,
painful cravings, and more
trite, wrought,
                and overburdened

poetry, leaves you semi-supine
with a leg kicked outwards, arms
clutching pillows *(no bodies)* /

                dead eyes smiling,
        dead friends dancing
across the blackened screen of
wee-hour eyelid insides, it's

a sky for feeling pensive under,
an atmosphere for regretfulness,

a dream where nobody has hands
so nobody can clap, a dream where
nobody has mouths so nobody
can get on with their life, a dream

where silence feels formidable,
feels like grace
                and god is a boy
                selling cigarettes
                by the pound.

KEEPING HANDS ON THE DISCONNECT BETWEEN GHOSTS

the survivors of doomsday medicine
look me in the eye, all gunked-up and
backwards, leaving their feet to keep

reeling in the wake / my wake comes
in waves, comes silent and on and on,
makes me feel like I'm grieving again--

so what if I am--so what if not for ants,
how articulated busses look like the
most elaborate thoraxes, harken the

wasps / they all died with me, within
spirits enough to keep a kill count
on colonies of anything but the bees,

so what if not for bees, if not for the
wildflowers that armchair scientists
say will save the day, say it from the

coolest nooks of the internet, say it
feverishly / and I lay back in my rusty
tomb, unwinding proper prose into

mystifying lines of landfill-ready poetry,
I let my chilling hands do the talking,
I let my lips come undone, I sweat.

re:

      I wish I had paint--
I'd paint the word MEMORIAM
so high and so fucking big
all over so much of something.
MEMORIAM all oppressive like,
like these dreams I have
where I hold this fucking box
and its emotional weight
becomes me / I'd let my tits out
for completion / MEMORIAM sits
on a canvas, spilling more of
itself than I gave it credit for,
MEMORIAM in paint becomes more
than the sum of its pigments,
becomes more uncouth with time /
with me-- and we toast.

TELL ME I'M WRONG / FIGHT ME

as the jellied current of the
river unwinds in my hands,

and as the rise of the tides
fixates on two points of a day

ebbing and weaving as if a
little lever is pulled and culled,

the pressing presence of nature
creeps past a mechanized soul,

holding court within itself and
broken computers look wasted,

filled with the marrow of copper,
tin, and all these natural spoils--

like two machines fucking,
it is an epiphany and a nightmare.

BROKEN DOORS ON SWOLLEN HINGES

"I've seen that light above me baby, and the rope,
I've seen that hole above me baby, and the rope"
        -   *Gowns*

it's become less of a dance
within a dark space and more

of a crushed hypothesis, a little
less swingy-saddening and more

of a slit throat reprise, as if
my neck could hold the volumes

of a mind and its slight betrayal,
slight distress in magnetic waves,

spiral, spiral, *calling, calling, calling*
dust and doormats everywhere to

come find an agenda worth killing
for, worth severing its own head

to forgive, absolve, and grieve again

NOTES ON MARRIAGE TO WET SAND

vows:

to hate everybody viciously and completely,
to drink up notes with fervor and fear,
to keep critical when the cool kids die.

to write a little bloodier for the women out back
who slice their teeth apart, they're so loving
they're all so forgiven and why am I so crying?

to scale up the memoriam hustle too much
so less it becomes an apathy, I study figures
for gold and his body is one better than a
dead fish, one less of a thing to deal with.

to exile shit words forever, to become more of
a sacrosanct punk rock that is rising, a moon
waning about, and her blood cozies right up
next to me so I fear her river-self, always.

to fuck less and cuddle more *(that's a lie),*
to fuck the style and hang heads on doorknobs,
to raze the rivers and leave dead beds for days.

to commit to an atrophied layer of salt and
tell it how much I love before I lick it to a null.

to be a better problem, be a bigger problem,
we're the biggest problem and I'm so happy.

OUT OF TOUCH AND ON TIME

my feet don't feel the ground anymore
and I'm screaming.

my toes don't touch the floor
and I'm screaming.

the wind
has eclipsed my neck
and I have not
found the right

to breathe
in this bed--

and I'm screaming.

I'm screaming awake
from a night
in which I
did not sleep.

so I'm screaming
something errant
about inland marine,

about sweaty sex
or obfuscating faith

in the memories
binding my knees,

these ghost stories
from richer places
get lost in the quiet,

so I'm still screaming.

frustrated and uncut,
prophetic and wry,

screaming,
having lost count
of my Halcion daze,

fogged up and groggy,
my voice is muted,
screaming.

I've counted the days
passing since y2k,
feeling *dark dark dark*
and incredibly sober.

I am screaming nonsense
into vacant ceilings,

and again--

my feet
don't feel the ground anymore.
and I'm screaming.

PEKARSKE HEAVY INDUSTRIES (SLIGHT FEARS, TREMBLING)

FOR EAU CLAIRE, MOVEMENT TWO (PART FOUR)

something dislodged in me:
I am still the shitty kid I was when I was 16,
same bastard girl that never stood a chance

it's like dredging a fever dream
in the air of someone else's living room, like
dirty laundry hanging in a dead breeze.

recounting a fear of memory,
how 2010 sounds like a low-fi picture /
sixteen was a hellscape without enough fire /
terror feels like a place I hung my head

I remember it feebly, I feebly jack it off
to usher in something poetic about ennui,
I prod sleeping ghosts for the spectacle--
try to tell me how this cherub needs to die,

try to tell me what I wore in the park,
we'd meet and tie together by the knee /
my body smelled like sharp grass for days /
my body--your body--remembers it gently

memory has its own way of fucking the style,
tarries and reformats bones in their god given
strata, we are so elated and the band is
so elaborate, I can't stomach it even now.

ORGANICA

so, how stressed are plants?
stressed through stems and
stamen-somethings I can't
conceive / pronounce, they're

all leg, all the time / you try
to stand for that long, you'd
wither and decay, too, you'd
let leaves compost, you'd
give it all up for soil and rot.

quantify-- how much less
stressed is my soil than a
plant, how much less of an
issue are my leaves / the
false fronds of my ankles

twitching and always out
of love with the breeze, you'd
find a way to hate ferns
if I were a lot of flora, you'd

lick black and brackish paint
against my stem / leaf /
flowering parts to choke out
photosynthetic must-haves--

an uneasy death and a very
stressful exercise in decay.

A GROUNDWATER ANTHEM FOR SLOPPY DAYS

break.

shit.

in.

half.

and question the role of rain,
spell death sentences backwards
    (secnetnes htaed)

for else a fear of god that creeps
and water that leeches upward,
finding its way to my hips by way
of wicking, we all came from the

groundwater / well water / brackish

slime, it's with me forever, it's
all I can do to keep a little broken,
keep a little charming, keep it
together / *secnetnes htaed* / or

flip the script for the scent of a smile,
the bunk view of a sunrise from
the hill that faces the wrong way.

aged
and broken *(in half!)*

under the same sky,

skip the sunrise

        and fall.

RETROSPECTACULAR

the peaks of your hands,
these serrated rocks I hold
as tenderly as unexploded
ordnance, as I unfold their
creases and pick scabs off,

let the piquing pinks be,
actualizing something violent
in the staggering silence
of an empty living room
with two unfamiliar bodies,
spiraling out of control,
sitting painfully still.

even as our ankles touch,
the distance is so cold
and motivating / escape
never felt so fulfilling and
rocks never felt so dense.

FORGETTING, BUT IT'S COMPLICATED

memory, only it's spelled memry

and towed so far from the thuds
in my chests, a timer on my thoughts,

how quick they decay, decay, only
it's spelled decæ, only it's decry,

only its water keeps constant, drinking

wine again, only it's fragile matter
waning again, we've been through this

haven't we--I would not recall--haven't we,

sounding off with the same stories
told a tenfold, only it's memry, a garage

by any other name is never a house,
a memry by any other name is not

a promise, only it's memory. repeated.

"TOO TURNT FOR EARTH"

Whitman could hold his *Specimen Days*
in his pocket, carry it 'cross his heart
as an atonal means of protection and hope,
a little book of skulls for whenever's clever.

so give me my *Shithead Days* and let me
suffer with its impossible implementation,
let me do this for me and my crayon-eating
human familiar and the animal in all of us.

SINCERELY CHAOTIC <3

unended sentences and really cool blood,
I keep yr steady hand for a piece of play,
reread your sad sonnets and think twice

before bringing you back to bed in another
daydream, our hair looked so much better
twisted, my fists looked so much more at

home when clenched and ready, set, spiral,
we're poorly matched but it's fine *(it's fine)*,
I creep towards defeat every goddamn day

that I circle your smile, play into your funky
platitudes, you're a hum dummer and it's
our balmy summer, we both hate your shorts

as much as I hate your really cool blood, as
much as I hate unended sentences, as much
as I hate you, so callous and sincerely chaotic.

"DID YOU REALLY JUST SAY THAT YOU HATE YOUR BAND'S MUSIC?"

of all the days
to realize that
my love of hate
is, apparently,
all abrasive
and a bit wrong,

misguided, or
too full of its
own passion.

said that I have
fancier words for
really shit things
and that I like
to hate stuff.

…

don't mind me,
cursing away at
rivers and homes,
I just don't like

trees or woods
or plains or grass
or certain places.

but I like these
feet on concrete,
the portal to a
city's soul is vast
and so capable,
it's vexing and so
sustaining, shared
across rust belt
sensibilities, trading
acres for decades,

histories in home,
waxing dangerously
towards love, I do.

it's more space
than it is place,
to be wary and so
cautiously brimming.

my sentience is
stagnant and maybe
I don't leave enough,
but I'll always be
coming home.

LIKE THE SOUND OF A FEW LEVERS PULLED ALL AT ONCE

a wisp of my soul
tears away whenever I see
a bank of lights shut off
in sequence,

overwhelming and final,
there's only one way to find out
if the lights make noise,
and if they do I miss them,

but when they're far flung
and I see their shuttering
from just enough away
my mind fills in the cascading
thump of discontinued
circuitry,

and I miss what was
never there, I hear
what never happened.

so soon and softly
it's dark, my mind is beating,
and we're alone now

AN INTRODUCTION TO VAGUE BILE STUDIES, TEAR DUCT HARMONIES

I'd rather not quantify grief,
rather not see it weighed by the pound
or spoken for by the pint or quart,

as it becomes more malleable and
gloom slips into closer corners,

see it scrunched into a ziploc bag,
moving and oozing within the plastic,

my skin within it, my heart buried
beneath years of loss and love for
people, places, and things
that just aren't here anymore,

until I've said *it's fine* a thousand times
it's still not enough to assure the
ghosts that it's okay to go, to abandon

my mind and memory, leave me
lighter and endlessly more able,

nebulous and fraught, decaying
and weary, it's overburdening and hard
to tell how much of me is still in mourning.

so I appreciate the ambiguity.

PISSING AND WANING

looking to see where your edges went,
where the lines in the sand were drawn
in haphazard fingerfalls through ash,

through the distillate of burnt up saplings /
last year's leaves, what fell and falls

every night now, it's some cool and
calculated abandonment--

> *we're some cool and*
> *miscalculated abatement,*

--we're so far from here or there
and the places we came from,
so far from those lines
we drew /
        I drew

into the tiniest pieces of limestone,
glass, carbon, and other particles.

WE'RE ALL SO UNDONE / IT'S SO UNDONE

catching, she says death is catching,
like unlit tombs and useless light switches,
yellow years for scratching carpet,
blue for a total fucking abyss of the mind,
my mind rocks back and forth,

doldrumming along, we conundrum too
tocking the ticks and fucking it all up,

> *I collapse in a pile of fake nails,*
> *come to in a pile of realer ones.*

it's not like I can talk about it
without some deep sense of shame jumping
across lanes of traffic in a warped record,

onto another overpass
we look, I look, overtake
an arrhythmic sense of
how bridges fucked up
my requisite isolation,

it's not fair that I'm this close to Bayview
but it's not like I'm on Coney Island,
or any other fallible prison of the mind.

we're all undone
it's so undone
to *collapse, collapse, collapse*

SWATHS OF TIME I WAS WORTH THE SUM OF MY PARTS, OR CANOPY CANNIBALISM

I would hide in the lake
        just to see where it'd hit me
        first, or later / if I didn't swim,
        I wouldn't drown anyway,

would see how a forest
could eat its people / feast
        on tree parts,
    fertilize its own roots /
    canopy cannibalism.

    it's awry and
        lonely.

    I'm awry and
        lonely.

I would hide in the river
        resentful of its
        easy-enough-to-see
            boundaries,

set mine accordingly,
obfuscated / he said
> I'm cold
> ~~to the touch~~
> to the heart

alienating and human
and really-fucking-flawed,

it's from the roots and up.

it's dejection or rejection,
I never told him which.

sad that / said that
I will never change--
> I'll just eat my leaves
> and go.

I SAW YOU WITH A GRASS HOUSE, I SAW YOU WITH A NEIGHBORLY SCREAM

heart hurts,
ankles scream
darkly
       darkly,

        emergent and cold,
        urgency and
            a void
        like spent winters'
        reckoning

tailor-made for
sun sweats,

how hot can asphalt be after
            eleven o'clock
      passes by,
throws its weight
around until

       I'm really out of space

    darkly
            darkly,

the sins of naive hands
become imminent

and clear, so
darkly
        darkly

every totem escapes
and all tombs are free

the sun is spent,
so happy to have found
its peace.

SOUNDS LIKE ANOTHER WORD FOR DECAY THAT THE DICTIONARY DIDN'T NEED

sing me webby
lies   to puke through
        my dreams,

         trestles for the
         imminent structure,

         necessary to keep
         plants from dying,
         formulating exits

         I need them   only so much
                                     as they need me

         I need it to be   softer enough
                                     and sad to the touch

         digging the relapse /
                       release

admiring the tides
regardless of faults,

so many words   spelled wrong
                      eaten without
                      cause,

    let go /
        left go,

    only so much space /
        to go around.

    trap my body
    in this jar and
        let it sink.

BIPOLAR DISORDERLY CONDUCT

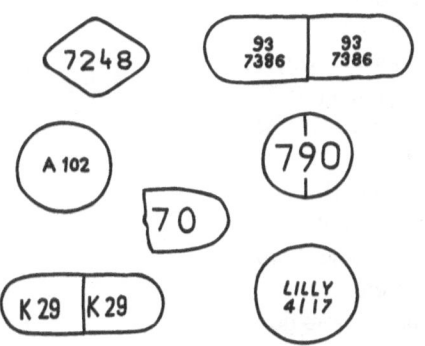

NOCTURNAL FILES, MOVEMENT 26

there was lightning
and there was lightning
there was smoke
there was smoke
there was sulfur
smoke, thick and green
wrapped around my finger
a reminder of a memory
I can't remember
where the lake is
where is home
I can't remember
where is north
but the green smoke
sang me a map
to a memory
I would not remember
where north was
but there was lightning
there was lightning
there was grIef
yellow and thick
like sulfur, braided
hair down the length
of my spine upside down
on the concrete
my fingerprints were gone--

            and yours were too

--soon my knees
buckled and scraped
beneath me and I
could not feel yours
your fingerprints were
your fingerprints
your fingertips were scraped
my knees on the concrete
grass was everywhere
and the lightning
there was lightning
there was grief
and my head hung down
there was grief
there was grief
thick, yellow and silent
there was grief
I hung my head on it
the pillow said goodbye
and I thought I was crazy
there was lightning
there was lightning
it woke me up
and I was the smoke
there was grief
and I was north
there was lightning
there was lightning
and I am the tomb

NOCTURNAL FILES, MOVEMENT 28

losing my shit again and
again, maybe it's just

a little more thoroughly
this time until next time,

gaps aren't just for teeth
aren't just for city kisses /

chain link smacks ringing in
midnight ear bones and

suddenly I'm convinced that
another something is dying

(*or dead, I don't know*)

/ found peace and poetry in
a mile of preparation for the

panic attack my body craves,
tell them that I'm losing my

shit again and again, it's
getting old now, wondering

how to satiate ibuprofen
seeking behavior, call me

with a thousand warning
labels and pin gold star

side effects to my esophagus--
it's what's inside that counts.

NOCTURNAL FILES, MOVEMENT 22

beneath stress, distress
and duress,

we writhe
alone in parking lot
stalls, differentiating
the good between evils.

when we wrote
the annals
of lost love
and bad translation

things
        began
        to fall
                apart,

so we workshopped
ourselves on either side
of separate clauses,

you became lost
trying to subjugate
the little love remaining--

trying to tie
its little bones
back together

on a night
left alone before
the last bar
in the city
shuts down,

alive,
and uncut.

SOMNOLENCE, A SIDE EFFECT

sans sleep, sans gate
sans simple step or sands of time
      without rhythm, without beat
      circa that year of cycling dark
caught glimpses of tumbling sun
at wake, unclear of morning, dusk

cicadas whining through night
at first light:
howling crickets
      too real for the surreal
dragging earwax like twine
in one year   out the other

tarrying in cresting sleep
carrying a woken body, an edifice
      sans entrance or
      mechanism alive
without the warning of watering eyes:
a girl astray, too tired to live.

always around the days die
around days, circa dies

HOW 2 LOOK MOST BEAUTIFUL, A SIDE EFFECT

e v e r y t h i n g
tastes like burnt pennies
       and your hair is wet,

      swinging in sequence
      holding shape /
           held in motion

      rushing just a little
      ushered by stuck knees

your hair is wet /
      why is your hair wet?

      / forever rushing,

      holding gate to bushes
      or the rim of the toilet,

      heaving - heaving a lot?

afterwards, it's the split-red
veins in your sclera /

        color theory sez
        the blood is a highlight
        to too-green irises /

        holy shit they're bright

        / watered and damp,
        american lawn eyes.

real flushed cheeks /
        freckles screaming /
            it feels better
            every time,

okay really / why is your hair wet?

you're not *that* sick / just stressed out,
it's court keeping / ritualistic.

this is for the guys who say
        u look so good when u cry

        sixty selfies later yr empty
        and it's raining
        / that's not why your hair is wet /

lips and cheeks and eyes and hair
feels the red in itself,
        feeds all flush sod eyes,
                fights a vacancy /
                a void and so

                your gaze is a mirror
                so see right through it

                it's not raining, but it's
                wet hair, dying eyes

broken vases pierce
throat sounds into sighs,
throat sounds pierce
silent air / broken, yes,

        and it's all porcelain / red,
it's not okay / but it's fine.

DEAFENINGLY, STILL, A SIDE EFFECT

      it's too easy /
about criminally easy
to imagine snot rolling out my nose,
like a really bored geyser, as apathetic
           as I can get
           if I try not to worry.

           it's kind of alienating
           to see myself so small,
           to see such whites and
      grays and blacks
and a few colors, I guess--
they're dulling fast and
I'm paying less attention

as days collapse into my lap
and I break them apart with
the stubby tips of my ugly teeth

'till my mouth hangs open,
jaw suspended in mid sag,
eyes glaze / nose runs, and
I'm sleeping.

DISEMBARKMENT TECHNIQUE

find me inside an algorithm
tucked out in square and
space,

inside of careful
speeches, where
parentheticals are
words enough to count

the spare beats
are broke-less and
humble enough,

and I am whole,
if fragments.

de-escalation isn't deadly
and our arms--

our arms
aren't untangled flesh,
are manageable.

HEADSTUDY
(LATENT AND UNDEVELOPED REVERIES SIGNING OFF IN 2011)

I paused to feel my fingers swim deep into the eye sockets of a discarded skull

> I imagined the drink,
> the swim, the expanse of all waters,
> or the oracle at the end of it all
>
> I wondered if
> there was fragility in the universe or
> wisdom that only belongs to finite sorrow
>
> but there was snow,
> and there was longing.
>
> there was a kind of fear that I didn't want
> or know, or anticipate.
>
> there was simplicity in language.
> I understood it when it called to me.

my fingers dug deeper into the vacant space and mourned the emptiness, the blindness.

> what my mind forgets
> my bones remember--
>
>> my spine holds the synaptic songs.
>> my arms are covered in toiling songs.
>> my ribs, a harp, play the love songs.
>> my fingers write the synergic songs.
>> my skull became the archival songs.
>
> --what my skull remembers
> leaves my mind nonplussed
>
> a caricature of sentience with
> tucked-in lullabies,
>
> self-medicating with sound,
> rubbed clean with frequency
>
> I hold it when it sings to me
> I carry it when it sleeps in rests.

soon the thing in my hands began to weep-- its miserable sighs heard only by the fleshy heel of my hands.

> what dissonance and disconnect it takes
> to tear one from its other
>
> to refrain from carrying tears
> weighing millenniums,
> crossing over from year to year
>
> barriers and dams are just
> cotton between bodies,
>
> the interspace negligible and
> the touches innumerable.
>
> no amount of latex can
> separate two thoughts from one another,
>
> no barriers stand to protect us
> from them from us versus them.

It is clear why I discarded it in the first place so I left it idly bobbing along my shoulders, still so curiously weeping.

DREAMSCAPE, OR "HOSPITALITY / HOSPITABLE"

"at the Pfister,
we're purposely protective of
very private people--
one time
we found a cup of blood
in a man's microwave
…
they didn't let us do anything
about it, just forget it ever
happened"

DREAMSCAPE, OR "RECKONING VERSUS RECONCILIATION"

is what I do a forever screed
or a whisper and is there meat
in the folds of the lines,
where the words don't go?

DREAMSCAPE, OR "NATURAL DEATH"

as I am, walking forward,
adjusting a watch
       (whose watch?),
stalwart eye glints and
reveries bleeding everywhere.

nothing happens.
nothing ever happens.

DREAMSCAPE, OR "NIGHT MEMORY"

"tell me that this
is god's country
one more time"
and I pushed him--
once for me,
twice for him.
"tell me
that this is
god's country
one more
time" there's
blood matted
in his hair.
I kicked him / it
broke his leg.

DREAMSCAPE, OR "BARBEQUE, BARBE-YOU"

     idea--
skewers through the legs
to stabilize the knee cap,

we walk like forced ballerinas
through locked legs and
     mutilated feet,

so fucking beautiful, my head hurts.

DREAMSCAPE, OR "NIGHTMARE WAVES ON A BROKEN BED, WE'RE SPACEFUL AND IT'S MORNING"

a dream where I am only running
I am only running, and I am fearful,
I am fearful, ushering breaths from
detached lungs, telling each one to
vacate, make space, because I am
very fearful, but I am running--just
running--to a fault there is no point.

DREAMSCAPE, OR "BEDDING / BIDDING / BIDING"

I spent a month listening to too much HRSTA
and boiling soup into soup dust, hoping for
an aeon of solace or a few motes of sanity.

my prayers for divine gin went unread
and white walls still held space for no TVs,

no river, no home, no roof, no roosts, never.

MILWAUKEE WAS BUILT ON SWAMP + BILE (AND IF YOU DON'T THINK SO, YOU'RE NOT WRONG)

ODE TO MILWAUKEE

I want nothing
but the empty street

and the wind
between buildings,
high rise lofts

and cattle lines
of twee women
at the doorway

to that club down
on third street

that everybody hates
but they still make enough
money to keep

their doors open
for a while, it looked bleak
for all of us.

I want to go back
to the Sydney HIH
building

or the razed tanneries
that flanked the river.

I want to eat
at the closed restaurants
my grandparents loved

before steakhouses
grew windows in their
secret dining rooms

I want to be blue
in a red state
and be red with anger

at the dismal array of
segregated
neighborhoods,
blunt racism that

nobody talks
enough about,
the city feels its weight,

while the people wait
quietly for something
to change and know--

to have hope
is to have lost.

I want to know everything
and fear nothing

in the gathering place,
by the water, watching
ships come in,

busses ship out, train
tracks barren outside
of Walker's Point,

take a dining car from tavern
to tavern, or out of town--

the beginning and the
end of the rust belt
is here.

JAZZ MAN SEZ

Written after conversations with jazz vocalist Dick Tate following the passing of vocalist Floyd Dorsey, Jazz Estate late 2017

jazz man sez
"I miss my friend,"

like I miss
my other voice,

my hand
hangs lonely,
these cuts
get shallow

and he sez
"he was older,"

he sees it all
a little deeper,
he knows
it was too quick

too catching--

death hit
in a soft cocoon

in one year,
out the other.

sez he won today,

sez he was lucky

and the machines
behaved.

sez he don't know
how he made it
across the street--

"it was like
I was ten feet tall

and bulletproof"

he sez
"I don't know

if somebody shot me,
but I sure didn't
feel it."

CITY SONG, MOVEMENT TWO

empty busses,
stolen purses.
evening sun rides
low on a bunk
horizon, empty
churches, stolen
dances.

stolen riffs,
copped rhythm,
without a downbeat
he hears his
footfalls but
probably couldn't
care less, just
feels more.

empty houses,
boarded windows.
two space heaters
and a family
of four tries
to stretch
time, to wring

the folds
of hours
and catch
oily refuse.

stolen dinner,
single serving,
frozen variety.
scientists call it
a hood phenomenon
damning hemorrhage
with fat
hanging
solid
out slit veins.

empty veins,
empty eyes.
life in an
aquarium-- some
fish are chastised
and the big fish
give them
no water,

they'll punish you
they'll punish you
they'll punish you

they'll get over it.

GILT, GUILT, ETC.

I cared a lot about wet meat that summer.
I drowned my head in a consuming couch,
feeling what fretting looked like,
letting it all overwhelm just a few senses.

today, the smell of Hamm's is a
heart attack or a homing missile, is a
memory stirrer and a bad time, feeling sharp
crabgrass and stale wheat at my fingers,
tearing it all apart. I fucked it all up

before taboo got the best of me
and I'm sorry, but only in a cool and idle way
that flattens time for no other reason
outside of my blinding and blinded guilt.

A HISTORY OF HOT SUMMERS

splitting the city schisms
into double-negative reveries,
running cool fingers across
chasms and deep rifts and the
valleys that made us this way,

> feeding / supplying the world,
> holding Schlitz-soaked ghosts
> and painting redlines with blood;
> somebody had to die to make
> us like this, to create all of it.

it's hard to feel any more light
when the blood runs so freely,
and the streetlights paint their
own picture away from the moon,

> and the sun starts to turn its
> blind eye towards the curbs,
> and the grass dies in solidarity,
> and Hope is just a street on
> the north side.

FICKLE FUCKER TEXTS A GHOST

sometimes I wish it was the old days
and we were really chill and evil and
still fucked up but it was 6 in the morning,

could talk about going to Treats or just
go, that girl had a seizure at a bus stop
and the city limo pulled up, the driver
was so concerned but it was always fine

she was always fine, it's not like anyone
cared, it's not like caring was admissible
in a wrongful death lawsuit, it's not like
we were anything more than the evil shells

liquor made us, it was 6 in the morning,
it was mourning or regret or really slick ways
to tell a stranger you loved their dick enough
to paw at it for a while, and all of us felt

like a god or like gods were inside of us,
and I saw the cinder for what it all was,
I saw the slabs for their place on the street,

I called out to the branches and my friends
called back to me, sang me a trap house
lullaby and the city went to sleep at 6am

FROM MKE TO SDF

I'm not as mad as I thought, trying to start
penning the structural integrity of a city,
glossing through all its veiny somethings.

keeping wind at bay--it's thirty degrees
different here--and these people haven't
crawled to Milwaukee yet, haven't been.

it's okay, who would Milwaukee, who would
Louisville, who would anywhere away
from love and the trestles of needing.

the quiet never changes, it's just redacted,
it's just a little more liminal when you
can't quite place the sounds. sirens ring

a little softer, the trees eat at the howls,
houses hold their charm in some casual
built-ins, they're not a novelty, they just be.

the dead girl's poetry still hangs in the air,
I heard that she wrote and she told me once,
maybe she showed me too, and I forgot.

without a belief in ghosts, she's a nebula,
without my own creed, she's a lost prayer,
since her parents took her paintings she's

a memory without a memorial. the ways
of living after death are so prominent, the
vomit on her bed is shrouded in plastic,

the mythology of her is tied to this place
and as much as I won't tarry it home, it's
a kept and quiet reverie, a sunken song.

MOVING THROUGH BLUELIGHT

written in ten phases while traveling from Milwaukee to the June 2018 Bluelight Music Festival in Highland, Wisconsin

MOVEMENT ONE

running west away
from a fractured state /
hypomanic / hyper and wild--

we're real and succinct,
we're running west,

the city falls back a little,
it keeps us humble /
it keeps me humble.

>   I speak for nobody else /
>   my only insight.

skipping town feels simple
until you are / you aren't
home anymore / home
is a fractured state

      and you've gone west,

outside of parallels,
I'm screaming
kept on crazy.

the city fell back a lot,
fragmented and wild,
and I pulled the south with us,
and we drove west.

MOVEMENT TWO

something crushing, here in
histories without salt and ice.

they call it driftless
and it's beautiful enough
if not a little hopeless,

        "look for a rusty windmill"
        alright, fine /

choices aren't fair, here
they're vague / we're vague
/ we're hopeless / we're desolate /

"meticulous" I guess,
nothing feels sure
and the heat is overwhelming

we're overwhelming /
I'm overwhelmed /
it's fine / will be.

MOVEMENT THREE

I'd like to check the pressure
of the air wherever I am

when it begins its bloat
from inside of my lungs /
they're filled up on empty,

so sticky and sweet from the inside out.

to talk it out / or type frantically
tangible as electricity, as hard
to grasp as a
fleeting feeling.

electricity withers, I'll be alone again.

soon I'll revert to paper
and scratch / it's fine /
maybe it's enough.

MOVEMENT FOUR
(handwritten)

bearing my arms
to make them cold /
keeping quiet to feel
a little more wary,

fracturing and falling--
now I am a worried and messy state,
they come together like
rocks, faltering.

an expanse that
I can't quite fill,

a containment that
begets lawlessness,

we're truly so alone here /
truly so far away from home,
feels fake / feels faint.

there's water / just for us
it runs without regulation, feeling simple
it runs cool / I feel heat,
my arms out, I take in the cold.

MOVEMENT FIVE

we've recessed enough,
receded enough.

light got lost like
the hills took it from us,

like hungry skies,
we've floated into it /
something is soft
but I can't feel it anymore.

soft enough to cry about,
grievously I reel,
grievously forever (it's part of it all).

> a quiet happy birthday for
> my favorite ghost / thirty
> and abandoned / my age
> at death, *grievously, grievously.*

no volume out here,
no wind to say no,
no loud, no light / crisp corners
with no resolution,

no windows, no monsters,
no, and I'd rather not like it,
and, grievously, I start to.

MOVEMENT SIX

Milwaukee was my mother tongue
until I spit it up into stars,

I've seen them now
for a first time for all time,
precarious and in reach,

solace in their space above home,
in their erasure in
cityscape scopes and strata.

eclipsed in light,
they choke in my little world.

I feel the reverie for them
in lossless light / a cabin glows
in manufactured starlight

the same stuff the stars do,
it's far from unfamiliar /
just speaking another tongue.

MOVEMENT SEVEN

we're alone now,
we're alone now.

light and wild / but
now it means something.

MOVEMENT EIGHT

"the water's receding"
and nothing else stuck with me
from the center of that song,

meticulous is right, tenuous,
pensive and a little lost.
we don't play that part anymore,
but it's poignant in a way / I don't think
we'll ever play it again.

as the old songs near an end,
grievously, grievously / mourning, I guess,
little shadow songs sit in air
here and so far / the lake
keeps them quiet, now, the last water
to catch their breadth,

catches up with quests and gods
seeking / sitting alone, I struggle
to place the next words, ruminating
on stringy bits of effigies,
keeping quiet for the sleeping.

I'll look back at it soon / and then
we'll lay to rest the part we never played,
"it'll sink back into the dust."

MOVEMENT NINE

fumbling through adjectives,
trying to explain my idea that
hopeless is a null hypothesis / it's not bad,
just without / it's okay, it's fine.

driftless, to be without drift
as if it's important to have.

stagnant, as if it's okay to stand still,
kept connotation away
from perception, it doesn't need hope.

it needs to be and to rest
comfortably and considerably,
the curt nature of trees and
all of everything they don't need to say to you.
everything is enough / more is too much.

hello to the sleeping salt,
hello to the hilly ruins,
hello to the creeping dark and the spill
of the sky, its pinpricks keep me gentle.

light and so wild, light and
completely still / nothing is at odds
in greens and grays, the bugs I catch
are the spills of the grass,

the moths are their own fire,
the breath of the wind is the moon enough,
we're feeling / I'm feeling, understanding
how to navigate this mutant landscape.

MOVEMENT TEN
(handwritten)

nothing howls when a sun rises / only sets,
wind falls silent inside light, I swear
it pulls a deadened timbre
from the swelling heat / it cooks.

so carelessly awake,
my sleep feels a city away,
feels irrelevant now,

or it would have been /
hadn't, though.

feeling was important / if it had to happen,
it gained its relevance
in the dust between cars,

retracts in the freshened
light that replaced stars /
cocooned away into the morning.

a few motes of memory hung inside of me,
a few moments swelled and ebbed,

an unstable bench wiggled
beneath my way and weight /
pressing the hills into my memory,
the clover that spiked the grass,
the colored huts that dot the landscape,
the cars lined up below *(they shudder)*.

so fucking alive,
almost afraid to leave.

"AN INSPIRING FIGHT AGAINST DEATH"

no hope.
no future.
go south.
feel wind.
eat shrimp.
cry a little bit
here and there.
find wind or ennui,
bury entropy and wrath
inside of a to-do list a mile long.
let well-water dry into the salt of the city
as the mathematician studies the erotic quadratics,
subtly eyeing the structure of love and the hope behind kisses,
why we lock our lips or worship symbols, ignore the simplest signs, hints
that it's summertime for science and the jury is on sabbatical for the time being
in Milwaukee, where lawlessness questions thoughtfulness, the trees are bare, the bodies float
beneath the winter ice and surface just in time for us to question mortality in spring's flourishing glow.

CITY SONG, MOVEMENT FIVE

in cold crescent water and
runaway still nights,
peaking in streaky pinks of
drowning yellow lines and
cyan fire after water--
life after razing: a symphony
of brick rain and the
silencing of home sounds.

with wonder and sighs,
opuses of unsound
cars whirring uncomfortably
while cold streetlights
dutifully magnify
what we don't want
to reach into the dark.

and city fortitude never felt
like a death sentence,
imaginative and bleak
like suburban sentiments,
just a bit closer to
very unfortunate crashing
that one wouldn't see in
a made-for-TV movie.

some howley things were
best left to woods that
don't show brick houses
between his dying trees,
curious places where people
seem to find something
like peace, only fleeting,
with stolen flower reveries.

but we licked asphalt in
rotten summers and traded
sidewalks into the fall, our
innumerable sacrifices of
skin for the scraped knee
reprise and relapse of
blocks-wide blackouts.

in this I trust: sentinels on
every block, light poles and
maple trees trading parcels,
telephone wire Christmas lights
strung about for miles, and
transformers blasting in the
night and we are united
by our power failures and
skipping heartbeats-- surges,
lulls, and nuisances for all.

CITY HYMN, MOVEMENT ONE

writing poems with
coffin-nail detail,
singing faint elegies
by the firelight,

growing up cold in shameless
nights, fearing death
by an engorged heart,
       not of health,
just feeling

like there's something
out there
more than star
more than moon
more than dead gods
       and decaying dirt.

WATCHING WATER, F-ISH MINOR

a harming calm unacceptably still,
all mauves and decay,
veiled secrets of bruises
little blood trails
streaked up, down
       --matters of perspective--

combing:
fine-tooth coming
opaque homogeneity /
gradual atrophy into
    violetwash
        bluewash
            yellowwash

taking its bow before skin,
anything but impolite

CALM PRESS, D MINOR (PARKING STRUCTURE, UNDEFINED)

in the shit-cast
        grease / air,
crater water, and
stagnant breath

angular ghost-clouds
        slinging low,
                waxing at earth

--all true signs
        of incomplete timing--

and our ears go pop
        when we go
                lower
        than expected

our ears ring
        when we go
                louder
        than welcome.

bodies fall
> in some cool,
> calculated way,
> rain drop / drop top
> so / so radios say,

with ferris-wheel boxes,
> Munchausen's worry warts and
> push-button reveries
> for all.

RAZED IN MILWAUKEE

"There's nothing left except certain death"
        - Phil Elverum

little more than tidal silence,
broken doors and sealed
thank you notes, never used.
there's comfort in the cyclical,
cold moments in the midwest.

every year my friends tell me
this winter will be their last here,
until spring vacations, getaways
spent someplace ideal, inspiring,
or at least less dismal, they go
chasing others' escape routes.

Milwaukee has its way with them
as everybody comes back just
in time to bake like earthworms
for another Wisconsin summer.

MORIBUND

for the Grand Warner Theater, Downtown Milwaukee

So what's it like to shut a door for the last time? What precautions are taken before the death of a space, before its caretaker takes his last glance, before he turns and walks away? There's the lingering "what if" caught in his heart; maybe someday, for whatever reason, the lights will be turned back on. There might be a heartbeat walking through the aisles of the theater, pulling cobwebs from the ornate moulding just as our humble caretaker once did.

When is it time to lose hope? In those days before indefinite shuttering, he'll have to take down the velour curtains (or were they velvet?), swaddle them in a muslin caul. But for what. No matter what the future holds, these old rags will never frame the stage as they once did. A new set of swags will be commissioned, perhaps in the same dried-blood maroon or perhaps not, and each moment of careful preservation will be for nothing.

It was worth it, though. For peace of mind, tenderly preparing the drapery for entombment was its own brand of catharsis. The thickness of each swath would only ward off creases for so long and gentle bends would then pepper the length of them all, but what does it matter, since decay will have its way with them first?

Corpses aren't even wrapped with this degree of reverence. The rabid children of the dead don't take on such gentleness while all but shaking the change from their dead mother's couch cushion. Even on the day the doors are set to close, the caretaker continues to vacuum the ages old carpeting, all traffic-worn and stained beyond repair, as if postponing one more day's dust will make a difference. As if it were worthwhile to clap the dirt from the rugs in those final hours. As if it were worthwhile to run a damp cloth across the statuettes and the pits of the crumbling molding.

We once washed our dead in oils and myrrh after siphoning blood from their veins. Maybe this too ensures that the body has one less day's grime before forever sets in.

We post monuments at the heads of graves yet in these final days the marquee sheds its letters, striking its name from the street. As the turnover of the neighborhood continues, who will call the once-mighty hall by name? Who looks twice or stares beyond the romanticism of obsolescence and decay, beyond degraded structures and boarded windows?

Soon there won't be any living ears that once heard the bellows of the grand pipe organ, its bores coated thick in decades' dust and solitude. Even in its most spirited days, did anybody look fondly at its crest and take in its continuo, the children of pipes with such a berth a mortal lung cannot comprehend its might? Who bothered to smirk at its player's mastery of such an out-of-touch craft? The caretaker didn't bother to wear a chintzy surgical mask to keep the pipes' dust from his lungs; he worked their metal bodies from their perches until the weight of the lowest tones became too much for him.

LIVING UNDER THE CONSTANT THREAT OF STARS

UNREHEARSED IN PLACE, TIME, AND SPACE

where
within the wet *(-ness)*
    of ravaging

set / spunk of
    unmedicated sex
    and innermost city drivel

hands off, of cobwebs
in cut time reveries … and
now my ceiling has
abandonment issues.

love / like cinder
    blocks
    and yellow school buses

    cut in perfect fours,
    your slumped shoulders
    look
    like they could feel

so right for somebody else's weekends

yes,
you remind me of Xanax
because this bullshit was unprescribed

and
you remind me of protocol,
of winter clothes under bed frames, and
of dust.

BIOGRAPHY FOR SOME-
THING DARKENING

s. pekarske is a crater's
worth of concrete pitfalls
        errant stone tones
        (alone and eye away)
from umpteen somethings
away from

        no, that's not it,

we're clinging to the last leg
        to stand on
        since those wind-wounds

pulling soul-oils
        tongue sweat--
        dirty

dirty
dirty
dusty
dirty

--pitfalls of glass and stone

and errant folk souls
        dust and despondence
        wheel-walks

        reverent sunlight
downtown good nights--

fucks and lullabies
fucks and go-beers
fresh air and frozen flowers
and apologies for all my brides

RECONNAISSANCE, OR HOW INCENSERITY IS KEY TO GETTING BY

we begin to recede,

revert to the floodwaters and
overwhelm from the root
and up,
        and up
                and out

        of the body and
        into the night,

        reeling back
        so curiously whirring
        in measures full with
        uneven beats

polyrhythms

it was unlike anything
I have ever heard before

I don't listen
like I used to, I don't count out loud

marking time is for partners'
ear / selves, is for more than
nighttime toe taps et al, et al

MAKE LIFE / THINK DEATH (THUMBS UP)

long lines and soft, smothered skin-somethings,
gentle shapes of slammed together,
raw-rubbed, sustained pulls and ebbs
left only rash, sunlit considerations
floating in bedside water and remedies
for this assembly of mort moments
lost to careless time and edging lilt,
hung air and her captured sounds of *whatever*,
echoes of *yes* and *more* and *morte*
and *muerte* and *mortem* and *death*
chided the house, its others in a passive chorus,
bent unwillingly as our bodies unmap
into tessellations whining, grinding towards relent
violent throes of gentle skin, of curving strain,
racing towards decay, unfulfilled, this skin
unbecoming and waning, simply arcane
pleasure-scenes of barbarism and relief extolled
across lamplight, across sheets, and rising sun.

WIDOW MAKER FAIRE

we were both so grossly under-studied for
this either/or of nerve-wracking everything that
came, he just next to me in apparent silence
without ever moving the bedcovers--

this little jostling, these strategic disruptions in
structured trails for mind wandering at
times pre-approved by righteous widows who
never held a contract, not before the sunset.

unaccompanied heart palpitations aren't sexy,
unarmed shrieking isn't always ecstatic, but
something erotic creeps home with me, or
someone erotic calls (and hangs up) as I
stumble from one room to the headspace of
the Ghost I Own™, the bed I left unmade, the
last cup of coffee, the lost bookmarks, the
three hundred and sixty-six ways I tried to
leave you, I tried to tell an adult or someone
permanent enough to remember me, but
someone isn't saved in my contacts, no
text message paper trail to fall back on, just
my widower-maker sensibilities, kisses that
death wasn't even entertained by for too long.

UNWED HANDWRITING

just like it was
        happily ever,
        a *just for fun*

amble to the
        pre-ambular or
        lax nature

of sleeping through sunset
and into the wake,

of widower practice and
pockets full of silver,

fuckery and windswept bangs
and eyebrow natures of the
until death do us no longer fun
into one another at the food and liquor variety

spelling *ess-es*
        with seas
splitting the ill with a kill in ingenuity

as the fresh hand cramp
resurfacing period,
uncomfortably welcomed
after a rushed penning

................unto teenage-esque
anonymities--
................or
--how many teas are asleep
................in spearmint

PLAINTS ABOUT PLANES AND UNDERWATER ANTHEMS

what's a memory
of a nothing in
a life that's cold,
        wrought,
        and vacant,

a little compulsory,
a little compliant--
        and if wind,
        then cloud.
        if cloud,
        then spoils.

        if it spoiled,
        then nothing.

        outdated
        and apart,

hugging memory, or
creating daydreams, or

finding accomplices
in paint   --
 -- it's easy to feel
like there's something
inside nothing

when its belly is
so damn big /
when our time was
so damn fractured.

...

three skies parting
in minor seconds,
he's beautiful and
I'm still dying.

SOMETIMES, STILL

MOVEMENT ONE

I told you
how I puked on a rose,

where the sun used to hit
and it locked itself out
every night, wasted days,

        told you how to
        simmer sweat

how to believe in
ugly prayers /

ugly people
and their edifices,
meaningfully lapsed.

they said
there's too many
overlapping timelines,
some are bound to end

now,
why it is comfortable
and grave.

MOVEMENT TWO

    held / felt
     to be true:
inalienable rites for
feeding the shit of stars,
today, for all days

holding this excruciating
faith in shallow, unwilling
palms at their sides.

the sound a tire makes
flipping itself over--

heads / heads / tails / heads

again, and now
quietly, as no one listening.

forced into stuck rocks,
forced into little winds,
tumbling, endless.

MOVEMENT THREE

it's all preparatory
basics, let's feel its body
come undone by its feet,

let's eat,
let's sweat about it.

levies broken and
sod undone
as I eat its roots for sport.

can you see my latent grief,
can it swim alongside yours
       (it's lonely)

can identity beget
pure, pure pain
for allegory's sake and mine.

answers say quiet and cold:
forever.

MOVEMENT FOUR

match like with like /
dead eyes with a death,

I made four houses
for carrying rocks in
timely movement,

so forget
about standing still,
how it means to tell someone
you're cold, I'm cold;
a body that shakes.

my god,
if you knew what I built out of salt
and its ruins

you'd know what this mouth is
or how its operation wanes
twice a day or so.

sun rises for Sun Ra
/ such a hard sunset to reconcile

when I've felt its
whole breath.

pains me to say
thank you--
it's just like a ghost
I miss terribly.

THE LAST DIATRIBE DOESN'T SWEAT THE SMALL STUFF

> *"and*
> *we're all*
> *going to*
> *fucking*
> *die"*

bomb / drums bleating,
quietly building cries for asylum
to the west, we wait for asylum
to asylum, a toast--

>   is it more than right or righteous
>   to sound alarms in the midwest
>   when the songs on the radio
>   are this fucking good?

so what
we're all fucking dying anyway,

we've become quite good
at this death game

this swath and swatch of ground game.
this swass and seasonal affective disorder game.

this diatribe of loose loneliness
grew tiring before my heart,
in front of its chambers
a speaker in surround

in lightning claps and thunder strikes

>   *but what about the creeping people?*

but the people, they sleep so sound in their beds
the people sleep so sound in their beds

so sounding
so sounding
so sounding
so sounding

TAKE NOTE, ALL YOU SLIMY FUCKERS:

there is nothing about stroking a breast
that is worth dying for

      I remind myself:
inside these outside nights,
away--aloft--from these
promethazine gibs,

      phony illusions,
      illustrations
with dying things, with dead horses,
long-legged Lincolns with plush back seats

seeded window glares, or
how the grey-green reflection
      to repel the sun ghosts
spoke my skin so smooth,
carried my chest so softly,

within winged speech,
impedimented, rudimentary grunts of
      not-quite-lovers'
gate, stip steps across my graves

and the tombs that I borrowed:

they've come to know their dirt so well
they've come to know what ash sees at night

    without teeth or bone-breaks

breakbeats or pockmarks
they've come to my heart in flares and fleets

we've felt so sick and numb from thirst,
    gulping when we must,
        drinking others' throats dry

with winter woes, sighing elms' frays

because
what is worth dying for
is irrelevant

PLAINTS 4 THE DUST AGE

get good enough and stay relevant for long enough that everybody forgets your first few chapbooks / albums / collections / whatever, and fresh faced fuckboys don't fuck with your catalog because they can't see their half-limp prose in your obfuscated early pennings and hopefully we can all forget that I left this poem in something once it fades into terror and tremor.

LIKE EYELIDS SPLITTING

with dark winds and too much space,
with decaying buildings still in use,

with torn up book backs along
with erstwhile harmonies fleeting,

within a quiet timeline and
a luxe and just parable,

the roses of moons precede you,
and the anger in the water
succeeds your form and self,

the trickling hang-ons of human
succession bleed the heart dry

and it still pumps something
twice a day, it's clockwork,

and it takes its time with tumultuous
and spirited ghosts in silence,

silken and very obviously gray,
making a tomb for every tomorrow.

ON DEAD FRIENDS AND HOODOO

she fell
like she did a swan dive
off a ferris wheel--

left the basket shaking
long after she's gone.

in a still breeze
her body shakes
and rattles. we watch,

and we know
tomorrow won't come
while her body falls.

but we still look for her ghost in the cornfields.

ORNITHOLOGY IN A DRY TOWN

we found a
bird with no
wings, just bones
where we only
know feathers, her
body clad with
what looks like
stone so we
just looked away
embarrassed

FOLKENLANGUAGE

the lazy tongue spat a train wreck:
a haphazard collision of stubbornness--
       of movement
--all aged and apathetic.

sacred mother tongue
left bastards to mutate
inside vernacular
       buried
by the speech
of the dignified.

for rhythm elsewhere, in
unmapped
unregarded territory.
unabashedly unpolished

across the bastard languages,
sums of parts--
       of parts and smaller parts:
--a shame to words
in stable shape.

word-children of crooked teeth:
the smell of stale cigarettes and Schlitz
washed lazy tongue--
of lax whispers and violent tirade,
to roar in discord.

the bastions of oral tradition
never wondered.

the bellows of men never cared.

in chorus with other bastards.
anti-prodigies, in rhythm
paving the streets of low language
with their bones.
fresh bones.

MY BODY IS A FRAGILE STATE, MY BODY IS A SHIP THAT SAILS UNDER MUDDIED FLAGS

AND ON THIS DAY

so he's writing again
>   so he's been taking inventory
>   of the things that come
>   before night and such

>   of moments, collected--
the last time, the first time,
the rails and the bodies,
>   errant yelling with
>   dissonance, distance.

there's something measurable
about time--   sure,
>   always quantifiable

but the practicality of a graduated cylinder
suits him well, something about parallels
and lines   . . .   and I am making this up

because quietude has no name,
only a few inhabitants at dawn / dusk / days

because quietude is the smell of dust
without presence of age or adage

because it's easier to say something
than to do anything,
why bother?   trains
                                    can't
                                    pause,

                                    pressing
                                    play
                                    when I
                                    feel
                                    like it

might be worth its weight in salt
to put my hands to work.

HOLY

cum collect yr dust,

saved it for you
anyway, we'll talk about it

fifteen half-years later,
someone recalls a frenetic nickname,
someone recalls a poem

>'bout how your smell hung
>behind rooms you exited
>and how I liked it.
>…
>I hate these people who broker my heart.

I like to be sad on my own,
cull memories at leisure,
Sam, meet Sam, who you
buried in earth and stolen sweatshirt,

Sam, meet the lack of satisfaction that
comes with drinking from an
empty teacup,   there's no fucking
water in there,   there's no fucking
tea, you're alone now, you're alone now,

Sam, it's ready now, meet Sam,
meet your dusty lovers,

collect their pieces and fill the cups,
they're beer can cigarette butt shakers now,

one wooden tip
off a Black and Mild's back, and we're
screwing up the doxology, I'm puking,
it's Christmas, your elbows are so far gone.

I used to fuck in grass.
remind me, remember me,

I used to wear less and drool more,
we'd try to beat the car wash to climax,
we'd try to find someplace holy, oh no--

hang on to yr dust,
hang on to yr holy dust,

hang on to your spoils
and strides,

hang on to each--
oh.

IT DIDN'T WORK OUT AND I'M NOT SORRY FOR GIVING UP

I recall your hands when
        I remember you,

spindly and thick with veins,
        they'd twist in your lap,
        holding air or
other fleshy somethings.

themselves, scar-scattered
from just little burns,
        working hurts,

closing curtains in the expanse,
asbestos folded into rows,
stable as you never were.

I miss their place
        when I sleep, heavy
        on the small of my spine--
almost angelic.

how they held a drink,
how you couldn't hold your liquor,

it's vexing in the wake.
I still think of your hands
       so far apart,
comfortably away.

EASY OUT / TUNNEL VERSE

when you'd paint bodies
of atrophy and ego decay,
my listlessness in the canvas /
convex mirror wouldn't halt
for enough brushstrokes or
enough moments to lilt

through color, only the gray /
green knocks of sick showed
up to the party, to the times

of heavy prayer and unsettled
petting, it's less dark outside
than we planned in the city

it's less dark outside than
if we had stayed away
from how bodies glow in
the lighted exit signs.

"CAN'T FIT INTO THIS DANG CAPITALIST FRAMEWORK"

well,
crashed into void again,
not even mad about it.

thousand flutes screaming
out of tune and on time,
could probably care more.

unlimited, imminent erasure
in mind's end lullabies
and I'm unsure what I ate
or who I slogged off at last.

the creepy comfort of memory
curtailing itself over and over,
erases all my freaky recalls.

…

now my blood becomes a
poison swamp, I'm unsure what
it means, disparate and bright.

REPOSE / REPRISE

take me back
        to our fickle world,
creasing my corners and
reeling--
tightly wound.

you're taught /
        I'm teaching
brittle bone how to
break again /
        break inside time,

keep me in 3/4 and
waltzing, keep me
spinning idly / waiting,
        or waning,
        or waxing
        or what,
        or why--
the creep within how
and the questions I ask.

there's just too many plaints
for every day

I escape sleep /
you filled your days
with the sadness of naps,

/ you control me
by the hour /

/ toss me nighttime
by the pound /

silent, and deafening,
quiet, and painful,
      the lights go dark
      and I begin to forget your name.

A BRIEF BRUSH WITH SENTIMENTALITY

before rendering your memory
as a void in my consciousness,
I tucked away your name, replaced it
with a pregnant pause.

in silence,
you are always at the tip
        of my native tongue.

COLLAPSE IN SEVERAL MOVEMENTS

"And by the time the snow is melting they always find four or five bodies hanging by belts from the train trestles, or in empty parking lots, slit wrists turning what's left of the snow into cherry slushy."

- *Reaching Quiet*

unraveling
at the speed of light in a dark place,
simple sinew of my life
coming undone without
virtue or decorum,

uncaring and relentless,
pieces of me drop and scatter
through floorboard planks and
into the tiny portals to hell they go,

they're so undone / I'm so undone /
unfinished business hangs still,
unmoving as the day I set it free,

lets its skinny arms hang /
lets intent hang / we're all hanging /

regretting, it's all regretting,
sidestepping and missing the point,

I missed the point, I missed the boat
only it's a barge,   sinking
only it's my heart,   breaking

again and so softly now, just a little *more*
and we'd have seen it happen,
but my resolve died in a slow and sacred way,
quitting before I become a quitter,
dying before I become the dead,
it's the easiest goodbye I've ever had /
it's the slowest goodbye I've ever had.

EXERCISES IN CREEPY TEETHMARKS

failing to play into
the gracenotes of acquaintance,
        these supplementary /
        unnecessary ornaments,
excess among strands of staffs
rhythm, I guess, or tireless beats

weather-worn ostinatos whipping
among a few sighed cues,
        20 questions, all asking:
        what do you want to do to me

what do you want
what do you want, what did you want
        where did you come from, *I don't care*
        this / you / it isn't careless so much as it is
reactive and so genuinely human
before teethmarks and waning

our strangers' fear of cold bodies,
clamoring at zippers,
meeting skin with skin, tripping
        over new things and parts
        with unfamiliar dimples

what do you want:
to blindly tie sailors knots in time,
to get lost in the tussle, to transform pain
        with want and should, try and wait,
to catch grip, to bend necks, arch backs
        with fistfulls of auburn tangles,
restrain, release, refrain-- and now I'm breathless
        with arrowhead elbows
running along the central ridges, across discs
rubbing so wildly out of control, so brash

as to control my breath, to become my neck
to break through to my scalp
        with too-sharp nails
to be the tin can, razor-edges, mangled steel,
to be the pangs of *this'll hurt tomorrow*
        fuck it

because eye contact is overrated

LITTLE LITANIES FOR SMALL GODS EVERYWHERE

I wanna pierce the pink of you and see how
it all drips out, it's all of you in the skin of
a thousand oranges as if that pulp will

protect you, protect your potion and being,
let it juice and drip so effortlessly while a
jet black, black, *black* coat hangs off the
shoulders so reposed and so fucking gently.

I'm a tooth guy, I'm into it and want to talk
about that, I want to talk about how your
fetid smile makes me feel like hot plaque
roasting in a fevering mouth, makes me feel

like a small god, like I'm in charge of quiet
but only until after sunset, it's like the veins
of a sundial are falling apart and I am enough

of a reason to shut the whole city down, shut
the whole neighborhood down, shut the whole
street down and black out the sky, it's forever.

LIGHT + WILD

I pray for the fork
in the road, that
its attention stays
divide and vast.

its tines are too
short for focus,
sprawling and wry,
pulling peace
from the fracture--

a party to the
collapse, it's fine,
it's fine, and we're
here for decay,

divvying sins and
sway, separate
slides for all my
peers and all of
their pressures.

ASH WEDNESDAY

she pulls on a cigarette,
blowing smoke through her hair, flicking
nervously until the waning flame
burns out: first, the tobacco
        turns to flame,
        turns to ash,
        turns to dust.

she buries an index finger into
the paper coffin of saint nicotine,
fresh soot digs into the space
between fingernails and virgin skin.

her blackened hand is risen,
her hair reeks of smoke and sweat.
she marks a petite, ashen cross
above strabismic eyes--

with vacancy, she says
"in the name of my father,
the sun, and American Spirit,
amen."

STREETLIGHT LIGHTBULB FILAMENTS' RESOLVE

brash poeticism in vandals,
mort virtues, lazy hoodoo
        and our rivals
        copy our books,
        rewrite our records.

drunk on drams / flyaway nights,
moot-point bullet frags
out of motion,
        out of the way
stay the safe ones,
no eyes behind all heads.

a distance: hindsight,
all 20/20 in orange-red-blue,
becomes utopic in a while

        mazy streets
        curl fingertips
        serrated, because we had to--

somebody had to go and we do too.

A COFFIN NAIL

with the precision
needed to replace
a single thread from
a broken sweatshirt I
am overwriting the
unnamed *yous* from
heavy prose and
reticulated poetry,
yanking reference
and reverence from
all of its bloated
nightmares and the
bone-thoughts stuck
and curtailed next
to hints of you and
yours and y'alls and
all the ghosts I have
laid to sleep before
2018 happened and
memory became
kind of cool again.

FOR KRIS, MOVEMENT THREE

"The shock-- sounds from a hollow box. A corner to dive in. I touched their misery, he just went to sleep. An exhalation of cold breath."

- *Circle Takes the Square*

in a moment
of wishful thinking:

may the spirit split
when the body is
wilted and cold

to be absorbed
beneath the skin

proportionally

to the love lost
in the past
of the decedent.

everybody left
here in your wake

could use a little
of the lightness
that you gave us

in life, in death.

*WITH
REGARDS
TO*

PREVIOUSLY SEEN

"The Last Diatribe Doesn't Sweat the Small Stuff" (previously "The Last Diatribe on the Island Doesn't Sweat the Small Stuff") and "Unwed Handwriting" (previously "POEMS I WAS OBVIOUSLY TOO DRUNK TO WRITE WELL")
Issue #20
Five:2:One, Print - 2018

"Ode to Milwaukee," "Ash Wednesday," "Folkenlanguage," "Out of Touch and On Time," "Citysong Movement 2" (previously "Citysong II")
Return to the Gathering Place of the Waters
Vegetarian Alcoholic Press, Print - 2017

"Calm-Press D Minor (Parking Structure, Undefined)," "Watching Water f-ish Minor"
Undine
Most Pulp Press, Print - 2017

"And on this Day"
Wisconsin's Best Emerging Poets
Z Publishing House," Print - 2017

"Ornithology in a Dry Town"
Brawler Lit, Digital - 2012

EPIGRAPHS

"Hang On To Each Other"
A Silver Mount Zion / *Horses in the Sky*, 2005

"A Little Titanic"
Why / *Oaklandazulasylum*, 2003

"Rope"
Gowns / *Red State*, 2007

"Monolith.wav"
Cairns / unreleased, 2017

"The Moon"
The Microphones / *The Glow Pt. 2*, 2001

"Broken Crow"
Reaching Quiet / *In the Shadow of the Living Room - Slashed Tire Reprise*, 2002

"Interview at the Ruins"
Circle Takes the Square / *As The Roots Undo*, 2004

THANKS BE

M. Safavi, M. Baldry, M. Wilson, J. Kinder, S. Johnson
For everything

B. Cardenas, R. Harrison, D. Harriell
For hope and poetry, 2010 to present

F. La Force
Unconditional belief / feeding my inner control freak

Var Gallery / J. Hintz, C. Ossers
For letting me practice chaos studies behind a pull-out wall

Cairns / J. Larkin, C. Conway, E. Chapman, E. Smith
It's helped

B. Thoreau and S. Kurter
For life

Chelsea Velaga
Cover and section art

Joe Kirschling
Bio Photo

Milwaukee
For your sorrows

Kris Sukup
Favorite ghost

RE: SAM PEKARSKE

Born / razed in Milwaukee and won't shut up about it. Tends to a small graveyard of musical instruments and runs a few reading series on the side. No MFA, no PhD, no gods, no masters, xoxo.

POST-CREDITS AFTERCARE

*"it's cold enough tonight that
all of Milwaukee is a morgue"*

>and from all that I stand to gain,
>I'm your coroner, baby.
>
>we live in the space between
>broken glasses of brokered gin,
>shattered window collateral,
>
>and these skinny skinned knees--
>your paint-by-numbers sprayed
>across the bed sheets.

a first date reverie, nightmares:
*"my god is gold, my cock is silver,
and commodities are on the rise tonight"*

>and we're hedging bets
>on a downward spiral,
>futures so far as tomorrow.

keeping these quips for a balmy summer   *(?)*

holding these skulls for the creep of winter   *(?)*

chaos in chorus, sing me more--
you've already put the ass in asphalt /
told me about your slick in the city

> *(it's dark out here*
> *it's twenty below*
>
> > *it's indiscriminate mornings*
> > *it's ineptitude by brunch enough*
>
> *it's a history of rust and stuff*
> *inside couches, inside and whole)*

the sweater that cuts into the city's cusps
fails the sweet of my skin
and blood dried open again, spit aside,
culling the feeding longing /
feeding the freeing darkly.

it sits inside my thighs / you sink so saintly /
we sing so swimmingly / hum so electric /

it's like these sockets inside me
want the lead of your something,

like bones beget bones
like you beget me, it's fine.

take care.

www.ingramcontent.com/pod-product-compliance
Lightning Source LLC
Chambersburg PA
CBHW020413080526
44584CB00014B/1306